# SCRAPMAN

CAROLYN BEAR

Illustrated by John Prater

PACIFIC
LEARNING

© 2001 Pacific Learning
© 1996 Written by **Carolyn Bear**
Illustrated by **John Prater**
US Edit by **Alison Auch**

This Americanized Edition of *Scrapman*, originally
published in English in 1996, is published by
arrangement with Oxford University Press.

05 04 03 02 01
10 9 8 7 6 5 4 3 2 1

Published by
**Pacific Learning**
P.O. Box 2723
Huntington Beach, CA 92647-0723
www.pacificlearning.com

ISBN: 1-59055-008-0
PL-7304

# Contents

# Chapter One

Winston was the owner of a junkyard. People brought him broken stoves and pieces of rusty scrap metal and old, worn-out cars. He had a machine that could crush a car until it was no bigger than a TV set.

Before Winston ever crushed anything, he would check to see if there were any parts worth keeping.

He had a big shed full of useful things that he had saved. The only problem was... what was he going to do with them?

Winston liked to go into his shed after work and putter around. He took things apart with his screwdriver and put the useful parts together with other useful parts from other things.

One night, he was trying to attach the usable parts saved from a broken cellular phone into the working part of an ancient washing machine. Suddenly he noticed something. The way he had put them together looked just like a face... and this face seemed to be looking back at him.

That's how he first got the idea for making Scrapman.

Once he'd gotten the idea, he couldn't get it out of his head. He spent every spare minute he had in the shed. He was working on what was to be the most incredible mechanical man anyone had ever made.

He made Scrapman with arms that could reach much farther than an ordinary person's.

He gave him legs that could stretch out as long as stilts when he needed to get to something out of reach.

His brain was the tricky part.
Winston worked on that for weeks.
He used circuits from a junked TV and
pieces from old pagers. He gave him
the voice from an answering machine.

Then he had the most amazing piece
of luck – he found the inside from an
almost-new electronic organizer to use
for the memory. He screwed all of the
different pieces together and wired
them and attached all the
connections. It wasn't a very good
brain, but it was a brain.

The only thing left to do was to get Scrapman to work. For this final task he found an almost-new car battery. Winston put it right in the middle of Scrapman and attached two big jumper cables to start him.

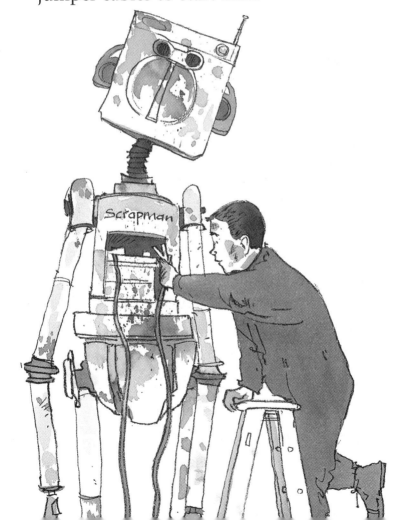

It was late by the time Scrapman was all wired up and ready to start. Winston was very, very tired. He wiped his hands on a rag and gazed at his wonderful mechanical man with pride.

In the morning he was going to come back and attach the other ends of the jumper cables to the battery in his van. Then, if he had done everything he needed to and had made all the right connections, he hoped and believed that Scrapman would come to life!

# Chapter Two

That night, while Winston was
asleep, there was a truly terrible
thunderstorm. The thunder boomed
and the lightning split the sky.
Winston was so tired he didn't hear
a thing.

Back in the shed, though, something
amazing was happening.

ZAP! A huge, jagged finger of lightning crackled through the window and hit Scrapman right in the middle of his battery.

Scrapman sat bolt upright and hit his head on the ceiling.

"Od ear," he said. "Ware ham I?"

Then he said, "Hoo ham I?"

You see, the brain Winston had made for him really wasn't a good brain at all.

Then Scrapman looked down and read what Winston had written on his chest: S-C-R-A-P-M-A-N.

Then he said proudly, "I ham Scrapman."

He got up from the workbench and stretched out to his full height. His head went right through the roof of the shed. Luckily, he didn't hurt himself because Winston hadn't thought of giving him any nerves to feel with.

He shook himself free of the wrecked shed and strode across the junkyard.

"Velly od," said Scrapman, looking at the mess. "Od ear. Od ear."

He climbed over the cast-iron gate and spotted some streetlights a ways up the road.

"Oh, velly pertty," said Scrapman, and he walked up the muddy road, leaving a trail of very strange footprints behind him.

The road led to a tall house with trees and a big yard around it. There was a light in a window very high up. Scrapman made his legs as long as he possibly could and looked through the window.

Inside, he saw a girl asleep in bed. "A liddle gril!" said Scrapman. He thought how clean and happy she looked fast asleep.

Then, in a flash of lightning, he caught sight of his own face reflected in the window. He saw how he was made out of old and dirty pieces of machines, and he felt very ashamed of himself.

"Y ham I so ugli?" he asked himself.

He was about to tiptoe sadly away. Suddenly, a bolt that Winston hadn't attached very carefully came loose from Scrapman's head. It dropped with a crash on the window.

The girl, whose name was Emma, woke up with a start.

"What was that?" she said.

Then she saw Scrapman's face in the window.

Now, any child other than Emma would have screamed and run to her parents. Not Emma. Emma had been waiting for a long time for an adventure to come her way.

It sure looked as if this was it!

She climbed out of bed and walked to the window.

"Hello," she said.

"L. O." said Scrapman.

"Who are you?" asked Emma.

"Scrapman," said Scrapman. "Hoo R. U.?"

"I'm Emma," said Emma.

"M. Uh," copied Scrapman.

"What are you doing here?" asked Emma quietly.

Scrapman looked around him and wondered what he was doing. The thunder was still thundering and it had started raining.

"Get ting wet," said Scrapman. He shook himself to shake off the rain.

CREAK… GRIND… EEECH! All the joints in Scrapman's body were making awful screeching noises.

"Od ear," said Scrapman.

"You poor thing. You shouldn't get wet. You're getting rusty," said Emma.

She ran downstairs and out into the yard and opened the garage door.

Luckily, there wasn't a car inside. Emma's parents' old car had gotten so worn out and rusty, it had gone to Winston's junkyard. Their new car hadn't arrived yet.

"Come inside quickly," she said to Scrapman.

Scrapman almost had to fold himself in half to get into the garage, but inside it was nice and dry. He sat down thankfully on the floor.

Emma dried him off as much as she could with an old rag. Then she found an oil can and oiled his joints so that they stopped squeaking.

"Oh, tank U," said Scrapman, stretching out his legs and arms. "Tank U., M. Uh."

Emma shook her head.

"Poor Scrapman," she said. "Nobody will ever understand you if you keep talking like that. You really need to learn to talk like a human being."

"Like a hu mung bean?" asked Scrapman.

"No," said Emma. "A human being."

"Od ear," said Scrapman.

"It's not 'od ear'," said Emma. "It's 'oh dear'."

"Oh dear," said Scrapman carefully. "Tank U., M. Uh."

Then he tried it faster. "Oh dear. Oh dear. Oh dear. Od ear. Od ear." Then he sighed. "Od ear."

"Poor Scrapman," said Emma. "Just keep practicing until you get it right."

She went on, "You know, you can't stay here forever. Can't you remember where you came from? Or who you belong to?"

Scrapman searched his poor brain, but he couldn't remember anything.

"I dun no," said Scrapman sadly. It's terrible not to know where you come from or who you belong to.

"Well, wait here. Don't move until I come back from school," said Emma.

"Skool?" repeated Scrapman. "Wot is skool?"

"School is a big building where you go to learn things. You don't know anything, do you?"

Scrapman shook his head sadly. He really didn't have a very good brain.

# Chapter Three

That morning, Winston woke up and went to his shed, whistling happily to himself. Today was going to be his big day – the day when he was actually going to make his wonderful mechanical man work.

You can imagine his shock and horror when he found that the shed was empty and that there was a huge hole in the roof.

"Someone must have stolen him!" thought Winston. He called the police right away.

"I'm missing a mechanical man about sixteen feet tall. I haven't seen him since last night," he reported.

Six police cars soon arrived. Twelve police officers with their dogs climbed out.

They quickly found Scrapman's strange footprints.

Winston scratched his head. He couldn't believe his eyes.

"It looks as if he just walked away," he said.

So the police cars drove off down the road, following the footprints with their sirens wailing.

Scrapman sat in Emma's garage feeling bored. He wondered how long Emma was going to be at school. He wondered what school was like. Emma said she went there to learn things. Maybe school was where he should go to learn to talk like a hu mung bean.

Finally, he couldn't stand it any longer. He had to find her. If school was such a big building, it couldn't be that hard to find.

He stood up and crashed through the garage roof. Then he kicked through the door, strode across the yard, and started off down the road. Emma's mother ran to the window just in time to see the huge, lumbering Scrapman turning the corner.

The school wasn't far away. Scrapman could hear the sound of children's voices shouting in the playground. As he turned the next corner, sure enough, there was a really big building.

Lots of children were running around in front of it, playing games. He crossed the road to reach it and a stream of traffic screeched to a halt.

A crossing guard dropped her stop sign and ran for it.

People on the sidewalks ran for cover inside the stores. People trapped in cars and buses stared in horror.

"Od ear," said Scrapman.

"Od ear. Od ear. Od ear."

He hurried toward the school as fast as his big feet would carry him.

Scrapman reached the school fence and looked over. The children stopped playing and stared. Then one of the smallest ones began to cry. Soon all of them became frightened and started running in all directions at once. All, that is, except Emma.

She stood in the middle of the
playground and said, "Scrapman, what
are you doing here?"

Scrapman was so happy to see her.
He climbed over the fence and
lumbered toward her.

It was at that point that both
Winston and Emma's mother arrived
on the scene – along with the six
police cars, the twelve police officers,
and the dogs – plus two fire engines
that had joined in.

The firefighters unrolled their hoses.

"Od ear...!" said Scrapman. He was very worried. He and Emma were standing in the middle of the playground. The police officers, the firefighters, and the dogs were moving toward them. Inside his poor Scrapman-brain, something told him that Emma was in danger.

Scrapman could see water shooting out of the fire hoses. He didn't want Emma to get rusty like he had.

Scrapman bent down and very gently lifted Emma off the ground. All the people gasped and the children screamed. People stood back and the police cars turned off their sirens. The crowd was silent.

Everyone watched, hardly daring to breathe, as Scrapman walked over to the fire escape.

Step by step he
climbed, holding his friend as high
as he could to keep her safe.

"Please put me down, Scrapman,"
cried Emma.

"Od ear, no," said Scrapman.
"Scrapman velly good. Stop M. Uh
getting wet."

When he finally reached the top, he climbed up on the roof, holding Emma carefully in his hand.

The crowd watched in horrified silence.

The chief of police walked forward with a bullhorn.

"Put the girl down and you will not be harmed," he bellowed.

Scrapman looked at the chief. He looked at the fire engines. He looked at M Uh. He didn't know what to do.

"Od ear," he said.

Winston, who was watching from below, pushed himself through to the front of the crowd and started to climb up the fire escape. Everyone gasped. When Winston reached the top, he held up a hand for silence.

"The girl is perfectly safe," he shouted to the crowd. "I made Scrapman. He wouldn't harm anyone. I've come to take him back home where he belongs."

Scrapman looked at Winston. He
looked at Emma. He couldn't believe
what he was hearing.

"He's right," shouted Emma. "He
may look scary, but he's kind and
gentle and…" She paused and looked
at Scrapman. "He's my friend."

Scrapman couldn't believe that anyone could say anything so nice about him. Suddenly he didn't feel dirty and rusty anymore. What did it matter if he was made out of old spare parts? Who cared?

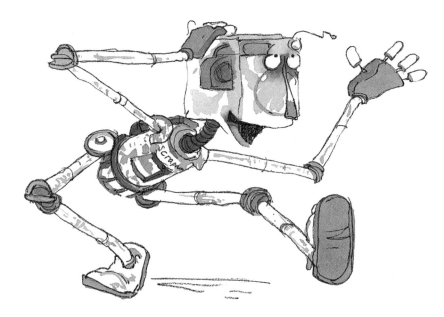

So the police officers and the firefighters and the dogs all watched while Winston and Emma led Scrapman back to the junkyard.

"Od ear. Od ear," said Scrapman when he saw the damage he had caused to the shed.

Then, when he saw all the useful things that Winston had saved inside the shed he said, "Oh, velly good, velly good."

He got busy right away sorting out some parts and pieces that he could use to fix the roof.

In time, Scrapman turned out to be very helpful. He could do all the jobs that were too hard or too heavy or too high up for Winston to do.

Emma came over to give him speaking lessons every Saturday.

In the end he became very good at speaking. He could even say difficult things like "automatic transmission" and "throttle cable" and "crankshaft," words that came in very handy at the junkyard.

When things went wrong, however, the only thing he could ever find to say was: "Od ear, od ear, od ear."

## *About the Author*

I started writing in advertising, as a copywriter, where I wrote television commercials and newspaper advertisements.

When my daughter told me that she didn't like reading, I decided to write a book for her – one that, I hoped, she couldn't help but like. This was the first of many books I've written for children. I now mainly write for teenagers under the pen name of Chloe Rayban.

My goal in writing is to provide books that are fun to read and that can compete with the many other things out there for young people to do.

**Carolyn Bear**